My Kids Gay And I'm Okay

Written by Karen Edwards
Illustrations by Rachel Dempster

Dedication

I dedicate this book to my children, Rachel and Jonathan. I am so blessed to have you both a part of my life and my heart beats because of you two.

Table of Content

Introduction

I've had this idea for a book rolling around in my head for almost a decade. One moment I am all in writing my experiences down with the hope of helping anyone who might be struggling through these murky waters and the next I think no one would benefit from my story because my experience is not unique or even riveting.

With the recent developments of legislation eroding LGBTQ+ rights through various state legislation I have real concerns and decided I will share my story. I hope this helps shed light into the LGBTQ+ community through the eyes of a straight mother and the message of love and support is heard.

Go
Wildcats!

Prologue

It's August 1979 and I was entering my senior year of high school full of hope and feeling on top of the world. It was a time of upheaval in the world. The Middle East was in turmoil. The Moral Majority was gaining strength in Washington and across the country. And according to Jane Bryant there was talk about a person's sexuality and sexuality came with choices—the choice to be straight, gay, or bi. I was a shy and awkward teen waiting for my life to begin and I am finally a senior in high school. I am full of hope and looking forward to my series of first. First date, first kiss, and first prom. I owned the world at this point and so excited for the year that laid ahead of me and like most teens paid little attention to the world around me; I was more absorbed with my little world for now. Within 45 days of school starting all of my hopes would be dashed and changed so quickly.

I first noticed cat calls when I walked down the hall. Teenage boys mocking me as others laughed. I just thought they were being jerks. I would walk up to friends and they would stop talking and scatter. I couldn't figure it out but paid little attention to this until I heard the rumors that I was having sex with girls.

Living in a small town in the midwest this was exciting gossip and it took off. Took off and spread like a wild fire and it didn't stop. I confronted one of the gossipers and was informed where the original story started. My sister was in a grade behind me and she went to her class and told a handful of people she kept catching me in bed with different girls. I was devastated and withdrew into myself. I felt there was little recourse even after confronting my sister about how horrible her behavior was and the kind of impact it was having on my life. She didn't care and I was alone. I never told my parents, and at 17 years old I didn't possess the life skills to handle this type of situation.

Every day I walked into my school, I was isolated and more alone than ever. I felt everyone was looking at me and snickering. Anything that went wrong, I attributed to the rumors. Every day was harder and every minute in school was pure torture. I reviewed my credits and realized I had enough to graduate midterm. I walked into my guidance counselor and filled out the paperwork to leave school as soon as possible. There was a ray of hope.

I went home and announced to my parents I was graduating 6 months early. My father was ecstatic. He taught at the local university and announced he would sign me up for the spring semester. I pleaded with him that I wanted to work for a while and then go to the university in the fall. Take a little break first. He pushed and the next day handed me my 18 hour schedule. I was enrolled and starting class the day after my 18th birthday. At least I would be out of that high school.

I started at the university and was thrilled the first time a young man walked me to my car and asked for my phone number. Even more thrilled when he called me that evening and asked me out on a date. I was suddenly living everything I had dreamed of for my senior year of high school but just in my freshman year of college. It was ok. No one from high school was on campus. No viscous rumors followed me.

I took the freshman Psychology course and sat between two young men who in time became friends of mine. Doug and Steve were their names. They were always together and included me in study groups and deep dish pizza dinners. Psychology rolled around to human sexuality and human sexuality discussion included homosexuality. I had no experience in sex and was still waiting on my first kiss (yes, I was and still am a nerd). I learned that within the last 15 years homosexuality was treated as a crime or worse, mental illness. The professor talked about nature versus nurture and poised the question: was homosexuality a choice as the Moral Majority was claiming? After my experience of being ostracized from high school I truly felt homosexuality was not a choice and that people would not choose to be treated so horribly by other people. I truly felt no one would choose to be a part of the queer community.

Because of my experience and the Psych course I made an effort to include LGBTQ and support this minority group. I had a small peek of how hard their lives were. There were articles in the paper about gay men being killed at local parks after dark. Frat boys laughed and bragged about reaching into cars and punching gay men in the face while they were cruising the 'gay strip.' Back then there was no such thing as hate crimes or LGBTQ rights. They were not reported and the offenders were not fearful of being arrested or held accountable for their crimes. This was 1980. A lot has changed since then but somethings have remained the same.

<u>Chapter 1: 1996 to 2010</u>

It's 1996 and I have been married, two children, and divorced all within 10 years. My daughter, Rachel is 6 years old and my son, Jonathan, is 4 years old. And I am a single mother determined to raise an assertive daughter who is independent and smart. My son will be raised to be independent, smart, and sensitive. Those were my goals for my children.

As my children grew I encouraged open dialogue about their day. My children would come home from school and ask questions about things they heard in the classroom or out in the hallway. We covered bullies, name calling, drugs, and racism. When we talked about people and how some people were afraid of others because of their skin color, my kids were dumbfounded. We even talked about homosexuality and I shared with them it was not a choice but it was exactly how God made them and we knew God didn't make mistakes. I told them, "People are people until they prove you other wise." This became our mantra in our household.

<u>2010</u>

It's 2010 and Rachel is at Vincennes University about an hour away from home. Jonathan is in high school. It's a Sunday night and I get a call from Rachel's boyfriend telling me Rachel is in the ER due to an overdose. She tried to kill herself. I made it within 45 minutes to the hospital to discover Rachel in the ER with charcoal staining the corners of her mouth. She is out of it. Loopy and obviously still a lot of whatever in her system is still there. Her boyfriend is there and he doesn't have a lot of information other than finding her under a tree after taking a lot of Xanax. He couldn't tell me what led up to her taking the overdose, just that he found her.

She finally wakes up and starts talking to me. "I'm bi," she slurs out. "I'm an abomination. It's a sin." By this time I am holding her hand and I say, "I don't care if you're bi, straight, or if you fuck donkeys. I don't care."

From behind me I hear her boyfriend mutter, "Oh my God." I turned to look at him and ordered him to leave immediately. Suddenly

Rachel and I are in the ER room together. I sit there for the next 12.5 hours watching her. She wakes up but just rolls her eyes and is out again. I am scared and I am so angry. My first born tried to kill herself and all I am getting out of her is she is Bi-sexual. All I could do is pray and when she was awake let her know how much I love her. And I hope this is enough to keep her on this Earth longer than my time here, and for her to have a happy life.

The hospital discharged her the following evening and we made the drive home. She goes into shower and her friend, Chelsea calls me. She lets me know that Rachel called her and told her as soon as I was asleep she will try to kill herself and plans to succeed this time. Rachel gets out of the shower and I confront her with this. She admits this is her plan. I worked so hard to protect my kids from other people but never thought I had to protect them from themselves. I ordered her to get dressed and we headed to the hospital in Evansville. When we arrived, I brought them up to date with the events over the last 24 hours. A psychologist was brought in to evaluate her. Within minutes she was on a stretcher going to a psych stay across town. She smiled and waved at me while they rolled her out to the waiting ambulance. The psychologist informed me someone would call me tomorrow morning with an update after they evaluated her. She also informed me since Rachel was over 18 and if Rachel didn't want information shared with me, they would not be calling me. She encouraged me to go home and get some rest. This was easier said than done.

As I drove home I reviewed my last 24 hours. Apparently my daughter and her boyfriend had a fight. My daughter is now telling me she is bi sexual. I assume she and her boyfriend's fight had something to do with her sexuality. That is all I could piece together at this time.

Morning comes quickly and sleep was about 15 minutes long. I am currently in school trying to earn my college diploma. I was laid off during the recession and returned to school to earn a college degree. I am in my last class of the day when my phone rings. I ignore the look of disdain from the professor as I run out of the room to take the call from an unknown number.

"Hello?" I answered the call.

"Mommy" I hear Rachel's voice on the other end of the line.

"Rachel, how are you doing?" I asked her.

"Mommy, come get me. I don't belong here. Please come get me," she pleaded with me.

My heart broke as I replied, "Your actions put you in there and it will be your actions that will get you out of there."

"Yes," she replied. "Mommy, I am going to group and doing the work. Will you take my calls when I earn them?"

"Yes! I will stop whatever I am doing and take your call any time. You do the work so you can be strong and come home."

"Ok, great. Would you come see me when they say you can," she asked. She followed up with, "I have to earn it and this includes going to group therapy and individual therapy. I will do it all and I will call you and let you know when you can come. Will you come see me when that happens?"

"Yes I will. I know you can do this and this will make you stronger. You just have to do the work and I know you are smart enough to do everything and they will guide you through all of this. But you have to be honest and do the work. Ok? Promise me you will do this," I pleaded with her.

"I will. I love you," Rachel replied to me.

"I love you too," I said back.

The call was over sooner than I wanted it to be but she was sounding like herself. I was filled with hope and was looking forward to her next call.

Calls came and I took every one of them. I went for the visits with her and her therapists. I told her I loved her so much and if the devil took her to the pits of hell I would go in there and put her on my back and fight the devil himself and win but I would not tolerate her doing drugs or have that be a part of my life with her. Addiction runs in my family and I already lost 2 sisters to addiction. If she chose this to be in her life, I would not be in my daughter's life. I told her if she chose drugs over me, her life would not end well. I also told her I loved her more than she would ever realize.

Seven days later I picked up Rachel and brought her home. I encouraged her to drop out of the semester at the university, she had already missed almost 2 weeks of classes. For the first time I was afraid to sleep, I catnapped and listened to her breathing, much like when she was an infant. The next day Rachel informed me she would go see her professors that morning and let them know what had happened but she was determined to stay in school. She came home after her time on campus and informed me she was still in school and would return to finish up the semester.

She continued to come home on the weekends and we had great talks. We talked about the event that night under the tree, what had led up to it, and how she felt now. I brought up the night in the ER and when she told me she was bi. She said she was. I looked at her and said, "All of my friends who came out as bi were really gay. If you are gay, I am ok with that."

"Oh, no I am not gay. If I found a guy and he did it for me, I wouldn't have a problem with him," Rachel said.

Ok. Enough said. A month later she brought home a girlfriend and there was a new ease to her nature with this woman that had been missing with every young man she dated. She was calm and relaxed, she was her true authentic self.

The spring session was over and Rachel had come home with the plans to return to school in the fall. We drove to the local drug store and I waited in the car as Rachel ran in to pick up an item. As she exited the store, she stood there reviewing her receipt before heading back to the car. While she stood there, I remember thinking, "She is so gay."

As Rachel got back in the car I told her, "I know you told me you are bi. I'm telling you, you are gay."

"Do I have the swagger," she asked. No but my gaydar was going off. I again told her about my various friends who came to realize they were gay and that it didn't affect our friendship and if she was gay, it wouldn't affect our relationship either.

"I'm not gay, I'm bi," Rachel replied. Enough said for now.

Chapter2: Please Don't Tell

During this time, my parents were still alive. Both of my children were crazy about my parents, their grandparents, and my parents were equally crazy about my kids. All five of us were a tight, supportive family. As a single parent, all of my parents help and support could never be repaid and was invaluable on an emotional and financial level. We spent almost every day together and if we weren't together, there were phone calls.

My parents were born in the early 1930s, survived the depression, and both were raised by their mothers. My father was a career officer in the Army and later a college professor. My mother supported him every step through out his careers. They were complete opposites of each other but their differences made them a strong couple. In their lifetime, they outlived 3 of their children. I cannot image the heartbreak they endured and they always kept on going.

My children and I decided not to tell my parents about Rachel's suicide attempt. None of us wanted them to carry any more worry or grief than what they already shouldered. As Rachel's sexuality was morphing, she always requested not to talk to Tootsie and Junie (the grandparents) about it. She explained she could not bear the chance of them shunning her and it would break her heart. She also added, it's a generational thing and she understood their views of a LBGTQ+ life would be vastly different to mine because of this.

My mother passed within 18 months of this event and we surrounded dad even more. Rachel would always say, "I don't want Junie to be told." I promised her I would not tell Junie and I kept that promise.

I didn't understand why Rachel thought my father wouldn't accept her if he knew she was LGBTQ+ until we were in the car. He brought up the Gay Pride Month and announced very matter of fact: "All gay men are child molesters."

I was shocked and quickly looked in the rearview mirror to see if Rachel had heard him. She was looking out the window and I could not read her face if she had heard him or not.

I quickly stammered, "They are not."

Dad replied, "Yes they are. When I delivered papers in Memphis, I was about 12 years old. There was this park and I had to walk through it to get to the other side of town and men in business suits would be in the park and a lot of them would proposition me. I was only 12 and there men were wanting to have sex with me, even offered me money."

"Dad, there are men who want young men to have sex with but that doesn't mean they are gay, they are child moelsters. Just like not all heterosexual men want to have sex with 12 years old girls. You can't lump all gay men into that narrow and horrific category. It's not true and it's unfair," I protested to him as I liked in the rearview mirror to see Rachel's reaction. There was none, I knew she had to be hearing this conversation but she did not react at all or look at me. She just kept looking out the window.

"Karen, I am telling you as a child I walked through this park at lunch time and these men were dressed incite suits and they would proposition me for sex. It went on all the time," he insisted.

"Dad," I replied, "if these men were gay, they might have been married. The park might have been a known place within their community to meet up safely. When you were a boy, homosexuality was considered a crime or worse, mental illness. I can imagine how this experience has impacted you at such a young age but not all gay men are child molesters. You are really wrong on that assumption. I have a lot of gay friends and they aren't interested in children as sex partners."

"Well, the homosexuals are bed hoppers. One relationship is over and then they are onto the next person. Just bed hopping and no commitment to marriage of anything like that," he says.

"They can't get married in this country. They don't have the right to have a formal ceremony that is seen as a valid binding union like heterosexuals do.. Gays can't get married and so when the relationship is over, yes, they do move on. But so does everyone else in this world. When their relationship is over, they might meet someone else and move on. It's human nature, not a freak show," I replied and I was livid.

Where was all of this coming from and why was he so misinformed? He was highly educated. This man, with an open view of the world, all my life he opened me up to the what ifs and how the world needed to change during the civil rights and so many social injustices he was a head of his time. But not on this subject. He was way off and so wrong.

He was quiet and I was too. We drove the rest of the way in silence. I kept looking in the rearview mirror at Rachel but she never showed any reaction. I hoped she didn't hear our conversation, although I am sure she did hear every word off it. And now I understood her fears that Junie might reject her if he knew. For the first time, I realized there was a real possibility he would reject her and I now had the same fears. She wasn't being dramatic, this could really happen.

I began to understand the Gay Pride Month. I began to understand the coming out movement. I never understood these things before. You're gay, so what. Let's move on. But now after such a callous conversation, a conversation with so much misinformation in it, I understood the need to come out to family and friends with the hopes of being loved and accepted for exactly who you are.

Rachel was pursuing her art degree at Rocky Mountain of Colorado Art and Design. This is a small liberal arts school located in Lakewood, Colorado. Rachel earned the honor of being the first Vincennes University student to be accepted to this school. She and her first official girlfriend were moving out of Indiana and getting a place together. I rented the U-Haul, we loaded up her car, the U-Haul, snacks were made, and our roadtrip to Colorado was great.

A couple of months go by and Rachel calls crying. The girlfriend broke up with her and informed Rachel she used to her get out of Indiana. My blood boils as I fight reacting to my deepest fears.

"Do you need me to come out there?" I asked.

No she replied, she would be ok. Rachel shares she is heartbroken and my heart breaks for her. Rachel quickly falls back on the coping strategies she learned in her counseling, finds the campus counselor and goes in to see her. I know she has the support she needs. In time, this will heal and we've all have experienced the lover who is deceptive.

Rachel throws herself into her campus life, into her art, and she is thriving. Late one evening she text me: "Are you still up? If you are, can I call you?"

"Yes, call me," I replied.

My phone rings instantly and my heart skips a beat as I answer, "What's going on baby?"

"Well, I need to talk to you. I met this guy. Super nice. He's an EMT and going to school to be a doctor," she says, as she continues, "He asked me out and picked me up and opened my car door. He was great. Is in fantastic shape and he can carry on a conversation. He bought me dinner, paid for the movie and at the end of the night, walked me to my front door. Everything you told me to look for in a good guy, he's it. But he leaned in to kiss me and it made me sick to my stomach and I pulled away. I couldn't. I told him he's great, that it isn't him. It's me."

There was a long pause and she finally said, "Mom, you're right. I'm gay."

I paused for a few seconds and then responded with, "You know, if God came to me right now and told me he could make you straight, I'd tell him no. Do you know why I'd say no? Because then you wouldn't be my Rachel. You are perfect just as you are and don't let anyone tell you any different," I said as tears streamed down my face. I could tell by her breathing she had tears streaming down her face, too.

"Really?" She asked.

"Really," I responded back. "Go conquer the world and you be you. I love you and you are truly a wonderful human being. Don't ever forget that. You're going to have a great life."

We spoke a little more and then hung up. I was wide awake now and reliving the conversation over in my mind. I felt good and happy she was finding her true authentic self. I jumped on Facebook to scroll through my notifications and noticed Rachel had tagged me in a post a few minutes earlier. I went to the post and right on social media our entire conversation was exposed to the world. I was shocked and remember thinking, "Oh no. What will my friends think?" I closed Facebook and went to sleep.

Upon waking up the next morning the first thought I had was of the previous nights events and my last thought of the day of what would me friends think. I was surprised at my reaction, "Fuck 'em, I don't care what anyone thinks." And I started my day.

<u>Chapter 4: No Secret is Held Forever</u>

At this time in our journey, Rachel is loving her life in Colorado. She is thriving on campus and very active in art clubs, art shows, and campus activities. She starts the first LGBTQ+ club on campus and received wonderful support from the students, faculty and the LGBTQ+ community in Denver. She is calling me and my dad and updating on each of her triumphs. Nothing is stopping her. Her daily call comes while I'm at work and I answer it.

I can tell by the way she's breathing, she is crying. I quickly ask her what is wrong.

She replies, "Junie knows."

My stomach flips and I asked, "Are you ok?"

"Yeah. He told me a story about these scientist trying to forecast population trends of the single cell animo and the calculations were always off by 3%. Each of the scientist working on the project could not figure out where the mistake was made. As they were brain storming, one of the scientist asked, "Isn't it suspected that homosexuality is about 3% of the population?" They agree that is what is suspected. Then another scientist states maybe 3% of this single cell organisms aren't reproducing, much like the homosexual population. Once they made allowances for 3% differential, they could accurately forecast human population. And since this is in nature, it's by design, not a fluke and not a choice but nature."

Rachel pauses and then say, "He stopped talking for a minute and then said, 'You know native American Indians found gay people to be special. They weren't ostracized from the tribe but revered as sacred. That two people in love who are the same sex make one soul whole and they are sacred and honored. And well, kid I just love you.' Mom, Junie knows and he still loves me," Rachel sobs.

"Oh, Rachel, I am so happy for you. Are you ok?" I asked as I cried.

"Yeah," she sobbed. "I'm good but I need to let you go."

We hang up and I quickly dry my tears from my face. Work flies by and as I pull up in my driveway, my dad is waiting for me in his car.

"Hey, kitten, dinner is on me." He announces as he gets out of the driver's seat and I slip in to head to one of our favorite restaurants on Evansville's westside. We eat and as dinner winds down, dad is looking at his plate and then clears his throat.

"Well, I need to talk to you about something," he announces. I just sit back and listen as he retells the exact same events I had heard from Rachel earlier today.

As he finishes, he looks up at me with worry in his eyes. As I fought back tears, I told him he made one young lady very happy today by the words he shared with her. I shared with him how she did not want him to know because she was worried he would not love her any more and that she did not look at his beliefs as a fault but that it was generational and she didn't expect him to change.

"Oh, that kid couldn't do anything that would make me stop loving her. Well, I'm glad we are having this talk because she didn't say anything and I thought I made her mad. I'm glad she called you and everything you're telling me is what I was hoping to accomplish."

Junie knows and she is still loved.

My daughter came home one final summer before she graduated from school. Her hair was buzzed short, she was sporting a few new tattoos (working a sleeve) and a nose piercing. We went to an outlet mall in a small town in Kentucky. She was needing new clothes and I was going to stock her up on the essentials before she returned to Colorado.

I was leading the way through the store, Rachel was trailing behind me, and we passed a couple coming from the opposite direction. They appeared not much older than my daughter. The wife first, followed by the husband. I suddenly hear commotion behind me and turn to discover Rachel had stumbled into a clothing rack.

I laughed and said, "Are you all right, grace?"

Rachel replied, "That guy shoulder bumped me into the clothes."

"That guy?" I asked as I turned my attention back to the husband and wife walking to the end of the department.

"Yes," she replied.

I walked with more speed than any other time in my life and with each step I took anger built up in me I had never experienced before. The couple were heading back my way and I zero'd in on the man. As they approached us my anger erupted and spilled out of my mouth.

"Do you really feel this 20 year old is such a threat to your manhood?" I erupted. The wife looks at me, this crazy woman and turns to her husband who has turned his face away from mine. "You knock your wife around like that, you fucker? You're really a big man, aren't you? You are a coward."

I was so angry. I called him some horrible names and my mouth was filthy. I cursed at him. He never looked at me or said anything. He was a tiny man with his own issues. I was an angry middle aged women with decades of pent up rage that was finally boiling out all over the place. Right there in the outlet mall in a small town in

Kentucky. My crazy was on full display and I did not care.

My daughter just stood there. We checked out and made it to the car. I was still angry. I apologized for causing such a scene and I hoped I hadn't embarrassed her too much. I would have been horrified if my mom had acted the way I did, I shared with her.

Rachel looked at me and said, "No, I know now you have my back. I always knew you did but wow mom. That guy was scared of you."

I reassured her I was pretty sure I was lacking any common sense at that moment. The very idea of someone intentionally hurting my daughter based solely upon her appearance left me shaken but kept me determined to always be there for my both of my kids any way I could be.

Chapter 6: My Friends &
My Biases & My Fears

It has been over a decade since the incidents in the first 3 chapters happened. Rachel is herself, Jonathan is just as wonderful, and I am a Momma Bear to both. I lost a few friends along the way but I have come to the conclusion they were summertime friends. Some of the time they were my friends; some of the time they were not.

A lot of my friends asks me questions they always wanted to know but never felt comfortable to voice them to someone. It usually starts like this:

"So, when did Rachel decide to become gay?" I believe it is a well meaning question asked from pure ignorance.

First I say, "Well, I was trying to raise an assertive female and overshot that goal and accidentally raised a lesbian." This is followed with light laughter and then awkward silence as they ponder if this can actually happen and where exactly do you draw the line between assertiveness and lesbianism.

Then I say: "When she decided to stop pretending to be straight," followed up with, "When did you decide to be straight and not gay?"

From women I get a shocked look, like I just hit them. Men give me a look of instant anger. Both say they didn't make a choice about being straight or gay. They just knew they were straight, never once thought about it.

I wait a second and then say, "Exactly. Me too. Can you imagine if we lived in a world where it was acceptable and encouraged to be gay and liking someone of the opposite sex was opposed, even illegal? And here you are being told you will find someone and love them and you are really attracted to people opposite of what society as a whole is telling you is the 'normal.' Wouldn't that be a hard way to live?"

This opens up the dialogue of remembering our first crush. My first crush was a young man who lived up the street from me in Maryland. I was about 4 years old and he was much older and wiser than me, he was in the 1st grade. I thought he was it and I can still remember his face to this day, although his name eludes me. He had dark brown, almost black hair and crystal blue eyes lined with thick dark lashes. He made my 4 year old heart flutter and I could not speak when he was around. My daughter has informed me she remembers her first crush in kindergarten and yes, it was a girl.

Then we discuss how difficult it is to be part of this minority group and all of the misinformation surrounding the LGBTQ community. I openly share I had friends in high school and college who were closeted lesbians and gay men. I never knew nor suspected. We would all hang out and party together. And as young people do, get drunk. I never had one of these friends make a move on me at any time while we were intoxicated (or any other time). But my heterosexual male friends were a different story. 99.8% of my male friends in the same situation would make a move on me, only to call me up the next day to apologize for their drunken antics…all blamed on alcohol. Usually most are nodding in agreement with me at this point. Not all but most.

My religious friends of Christian faith by now are following up with, "Well, you know what Jesus says. How about that?" My pat answer is, "Jesus says to love one another. A sin is a sin and is up to God to pass judgement. If God is so perfect and he makes all of us and he doesn't make mistakes…but the queer community is his mistake. Is that what you are saying?"

Usually they scratch their heads and try to quote from the Bible and the words like choice and abomination are thrown around a lot. I just stop them and say, "We are suppose to love one another. There are plenty of hateful people in this world. Love one another, nothing more and nothing less. We don't have to like what they do or even understand it. Just love one another. It is an abomination to masturbate, have sex for pleasure, and not to have your daughter traded off for a couple of goats prior to her second menstruation cycle in an arranged marriage. And most girls get their periods between 12 and 13 years old, sometimes younger. You can't cherry pick what you want to follow as God's word and pass judgement on others." This conversation usually ends with people just staring at me.

I'm more spiritual than religious. I had a friend tell me years ago that religion was designed to control people. I believe he might just be right. I believe there is a supreme being and she has given us the greatest gift of unconditional love.

<u>My Biases and My Fears</u>

While I chuckle and shake my head at my friends, I have to own my own preconceive notions and words I've had to come to terms with over the years as well. I have not always chosen the correct verbiage and made comments without thinking them through.

For one, as Rachel came out, I requested she not make out in front of me. I stopped myself at one point and asked her if that made me homophobic? She chuckled and said "No, that was the rule when I was dating guys. If someone wants to be overly affectionate in front of other people, they are showing disrespect for you and your relationship. The same holds true for gay relationships."

I did reassure her the cuddling, hand holding, and kisses I was comfortable with and that was not a problem for me. When you are in a loving relationship, it's part of the territory regardless of it being a heterosexual or homosexual relationship.

But the one thing I have not discussed with Rachel was this thoughtless comment and it bothers me to this day. As she accepted who she is and as she became more confident with how she wanted her life to unfold, I told her I had no problem with her being openly gay. To live an authentic life but I added, "Just don't go 'dikie' on me."

I cringe even now just typing this out but feel I need to be open about my experience with you. As the years have gone on my daughter has morphed into a beautiful, smart, caring human being that sees the good in everyone she meets. She will stop and hold the door open for someone, she will greet strangers on the street, and she is the first to come running if anyone needs her help. And my daughter wears her hair buzzed short (shaved on the sides), nose ring, eye brow ring, tats on her arms and chest, gauges in her earlobes, and a lot of plaid flannel shirts. And as someone might say, "Looks dikie."

Rachel is a work of art and she displays her art on her body and it is beautiful. The words "dike" or "dikie" are no longer a part of my vocabulary. They don't exist but at one point it did and I own my biases. I believe this bias came out of fear of ignorant people targeting her in public and attacking her. Seems far fetched but it happened to her at the age of 20 in a small town in Kentucky with me standing right there with her. I worry that she will be attacked while she is out because she is identified and part of the minority queer community. She is married to a wonderful woman and they travel together. I worry and most parents I have talked with, this is they're number one worry: being physically assaulted or worse killed because they are LGBTQ+ or "appear" to be LGBTQ+.

PRIDE

June is Pride month. My daughter and her wife attended this event every year in Denver until 2021, when radical groups were calling to show up at these festivals and shoot the gays. Really? What is wrong with people? This reminds me of a conversation I had with an openly gay man back around 2009 and he told me he hated Pride Parades.

I was surprised but he went on to explain: "Here is the gay community waving rainbow flags, dressed in costumes, and having a party. The rest of the world is watching and the misinformed idiots think this is how we are all the time. Just think if you looked at the Mardi Gras parade, with little knowledge of what life for heterosexuals was like and there is Mardi Gras parades going on and being televised on the news. You would think that is how heterosexuals were….dressing up in wigs, heels, fairy wings, and all."

Wow, that was an eye opener for me. I had never thought of that and I believed he had a valid point in his argument. It's now 2023 and Pride Parades are in almost every city and being attended by the queer and heterosexual communities together.

Evansville hosted their first River City Pride Event before the pandemic in 2019. I joined the group Free Mom Hugs, bought my Momma Bear pride shirt to wear while I attended this event. I even called Rachel and told her I was attending and I hoped to hug a lot of kids down there.

I went to my first Pride Festival and walked around. I had a blast, enjoyed the people, and shared in the feeling of love everyone was exuding.

I stayed about 3 hours and then stopped by Target on my way home. I ran into the cosmetics department and a Target associate came up to me and asked me if she could help me.

She's in her late teens, early 20s, fresh face wearing the red polo that identifies her as an employee of Target. I told her what I was looking for and she walked me over to the requested item, picked it up, and then quietly said, "I like your tee shirt. I am going down there after work tonight."

I looked at her, smiled and said, "Be careful. It's in a bad part of town, don't walk down there by yourself. It is a blast. I am part of the Free Mom Hugs group. Can I give you a hug?"

She nodded and we are hugging each other in the middle of Target's cosmetic department. I have no idea her name and can barely recall her face but I remember what she said next as she whispered in my ear, "I needed this."

With tears streaming down my face I whispered back, "Don't ever let anyone make you feel like you are a mistake. You are not. You are wonderful and you be extraordinary in all that you do. You be you." We hugged for a few more seconds and then I gave her more advise to have fun tonight but to be careful. Momma Bear was in full swing.

Looking back on this event, I hope this young lady had a great time that night. I hope she was safe and I hope whatever her journey is, she is able to have the love and support along the way for her to have the freedom to blossom as a human being to her fullest potential.

Both of my kids and myself have earned college degrees. Rachel met a wonderful woman, Bayley, who truly loves Rachel and lets Rachel be Rachel. They have been together 10 years and married for over 4 years. Rachel is a published children's illustrator and is currently training to pursue her first love of animals in the veterinary field. She and Bayley are thriving and still live in Colorado and share living a full, authentic life.

Jonathan hiked the Pacific Crest Trail in 5 months after graduation from college. He fell in love with the great outdoors and decided he wanted to live out west. He moved to Oregon and recently relocated to Utah. He has met a wonderful woman, Betsy and I am hoping to hear wedding bells soon.

Junie joined my mother into the next life in 2017. Both of them had a huge impact on my life and the lives of my children. We were truly blessed to have them in our lives as long as we did but with any loss, we all feel it was never enough time. Both are missed daily.

I'm still in the Midwest, in my small Indiana town. I share my home with my dogs. I travel as much as possible and am always ready for the next adventure. I have a great group of supportive friends. I visit my kids as much as possible and I am always trying to get all 3 of us in one place at the same time. This has proven tougher than it appears to be.

As I review my life I realize my greatest accomplishments are my children. There have been a lot of tears, laughter, and heartbreak on this wild ride called life but I wouldn't change any of this journey. For the most part, we are happy and healthy.

My kids are thriving as adults, I love the calls that I get from both of them that start with, "Oh my, I have no idea how you did it. It is so hard." I smile and just tell them to break things down into small manageable bites or steps. Take this one step at a time and you can get through anything. It might not feel like it at the time but it will happen. I am so proud of both of my kids and I am enjoying watching them live their true authentic lives. It Is all better than ok, it is a wonderful life.

<u>EPILOGUE</u>

When you have children, you have your own dreams for them. You look into your child's face and imagine what their likes and interest will be. You arrange play dates and enroll them into activities such as dance classes, t-ball, and scouts. As they mature and grow into adults, they become who they are. While you realize you had an influence on them, they are their own individual personality.

Along the way, you experience their "first" of everything. First steps, first words, first tooth, and a lot of first we cherish and commit to our deepest memories. As a parent I have come to realize I relish every first my kids share with me through out their lives even as they enter adulthood. First love, first heartache, and more.

If I rejected my daughter at the age of 20, I would have lost out on the last 13 years of her life. I would not have seen her graduate with honors from college. I would not have her first printed illustrated book on my shelf. I would not have attended her wedding or taken family vacations with her and her wife.

I have enjoyed every first my adult kids have shared with me just as much as I did when they were babies, toddlers, and teenagers.

If your child has shared with you they identify as part of the LGBTQ+ community, please remember they are the same baby the nurses placed in your arms all those years ago. They haven't turned into a deviant monster, they just shared with you one of their biggest secrets and now fear of rejection. They fear the people they love the most will turn their backs on them, stop loving them, and shun them. Complete strangers do that to them every day. Social media is even more brutal.

As a parent, you will feel isolated and unsure as you navigate through this time. Just know you are not alone. You have your own fears and some of the people you considered friends, will no longer make themselves available to you.

I have heard of families losing their church family and the spiritual and the emotional support because they did not disown their child when it became known their child identifies at LGBTQ+. It wasn't much of a support system if a religious group expects you to choose a side between an organization and your child.

While you may not understand your child at this moment, you can support them and need to realize your life is going to change. It's rocky at first but it does get so much better.

You have other look at your own biases and face them. These biases will be challenged during this trip through life and a lot of beliefs will no longer serve you. I remember looking at Rachel and apologizing for telling her as a child and young adult she would meet a nice young man and get married. I acknowledged how much pressure that had to put on her and for that, I was truly sorry. It just never occurred to me she might not be straight. In true Rachel fashion she answered, "Oh, mom, that's ok. You didn't know and I was a little clueless myself. It's all good." How did I get such great kids?

I cannot imagine my life without my children in it. I cannot imagine my daughter and her wife not being a part of my life and not having their support and love. My son is equally supportive of his sister and sister-in-law. I truly believe if I had rejected my daughter, it would have altered my relationship with my son and his family as well.

My daughter's relationships are our normal. I see the looks, I see the double takes and I smile back at these people. So does my daughter. Overall, all human beings are living sentient beings and deserve respect, just like all other sentient beings. Humans need love in their lives and love helps us thrive through this life. Love never hurt anyone. Just love your children, love one another, and most importantly love yourself even more.

Hugs and Love,
Karen

<u>Rachel's Thoughts</u>

With myself being a Millennial and seeing the gradual changes revolving around LGBTQ+ rights to healthcare, marriage, and adoptions, it's been so eye opening to see the progress within my lifetime. It's not perfect but it is a stable foothold for future generations to grow & learn from.

Growing up in the '90's and early Thousands versus where we are now as a society today is a drastic changes that I can only see improving with the new generation of Gen X coming into the foreshadows of voters rights, work forces and so many other valuable opportunities that were restricted when I was their age. The future for so many can be so bright & promising if we continue on the path we are currently fighting down. It won't be easy but with the right mindset ANYTHING can happen. Love always wins.

With my mothers book I am hoping that this is a ray of light to an older generation that has had to relearn a thought process towards the LGBTQ+ community & brings some parents peace of a "ah hah" moment with folds that may be struggling with a child, grandchild, niece, nephew or god child coming out as gay, transgender, non-binary or any form of self expression. Having a loving, supportive & respectful parent or family member is crucial to anyones journey. You may not understand it but you can always respect it.

Love, respect, guidance & resources is the best nurturing anyone child ever do as a parent. I was lucky enough to have a mother that valued all four levels of nurturing & has grown as a human in the best ways possible. She is so loving to everyone & has the biggest heart when in todays world that may be seen as a weakness. If compassion is a weakness then I wish the world would fall to their knees. We can be the change… You just have to be willing to reach out & accept the message.

We are capable of beautiful things… One act of kinds at a time.

Rachel Dempster

Acknowledgement

I want to thank my family for supporting my idea and encouraging me to pursue this first book. A special thanks to my daughter, Rachel, for giving me her permission to share our story, for the artwork she created in this book, and helping me use the correct verbiage for telling our story.

Thank you to my friends who I discussed endlessly this book concept and my hope of connecting with the right people who could benefit from my families experiences.

And to the reader, thank you for purchasing this book. Please share my story with someone you love and as always, I hope this story inspires you.

AFTERWORD

According to the Williams Institute 61% of suicide attempts among LGBQT community happen within 5 years of realizing they are LGBQT.

42% of people who are LGBQT report living in an unwelcoming environment.

80% of gay and lesbian youth report severe social isolation.

6 in 10 LGBQT students report feeling unsafe at school because of their orientation.

90% of LGBQT teens come out to their close friends.

As of 2023, bills are pending or have been passed in several states restricting the rights of members (or perceived members) of the LGBTQ community. Tennessee passed a bill regulating drag show performances, criminalizing "adult cabaret entertainment" that takes place in public or in front of minors. This law states these shows are harmful to minors. Currently the U. S. District Judge issued a temporary injunction because the law is too vague and is too broad to allow differing outcomes based on a person's assessment of what is or isn't obscene.

Florida passed a bill that restricts discussions of sexual orientation and gender identity in schools. Known as the "Don't Say Gay" law it states, "Classroom instructions by school personnel or third parties on sexual orientation or gender identity may not occur in kindergarten through grade 3 or in a manner that is not age-appropriate or developmentally appropriate for students in accordance with state standards." This was later expanded to all grades throughout the state by the Florida board of education. This law, much like the Tennessee law, is vague leaving teachers confused on what they can and can't discuss in their classroom.

The attorney general of the state of Texas is interpreting existing laws and states that gender affirming health care for children should be criminalized as a form of child abuse. The governor then ordered state agencies to investigate parents whose children are receiving gender-affirming healthcare and threatened punishment for state agencies and medical professionals who fail to report it.

The witch hunt continues. It's time to stop this and live in harmony and protect our minority LGBTQ community.

www.ingramcontent.com/pod-product-compliance
Lightning Source LLC
Chambersburg PA
CBHW050609160726
48003CB00003B/1111